# Kitten Love Colouring Book

Morgan Fitzsimons

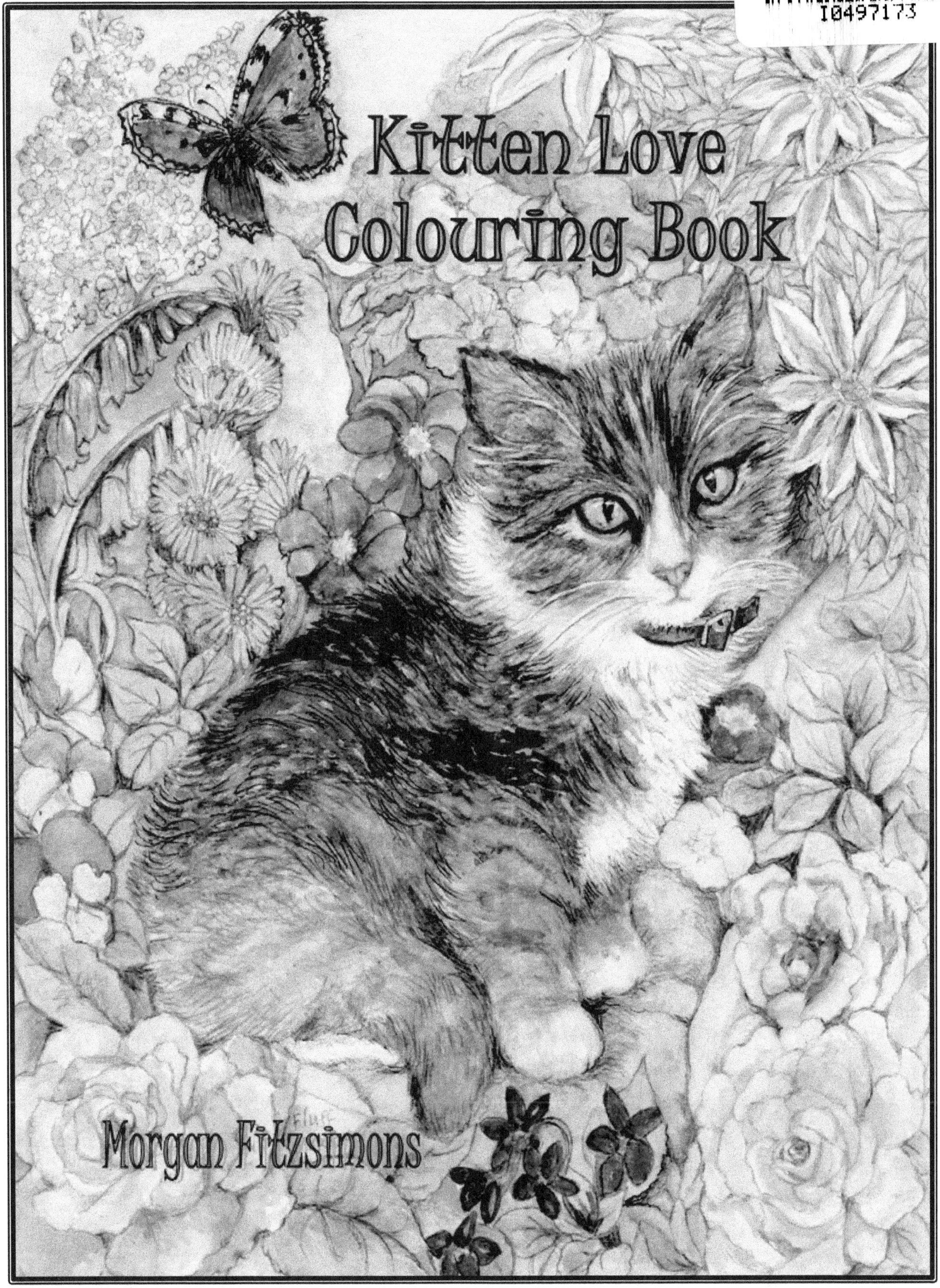

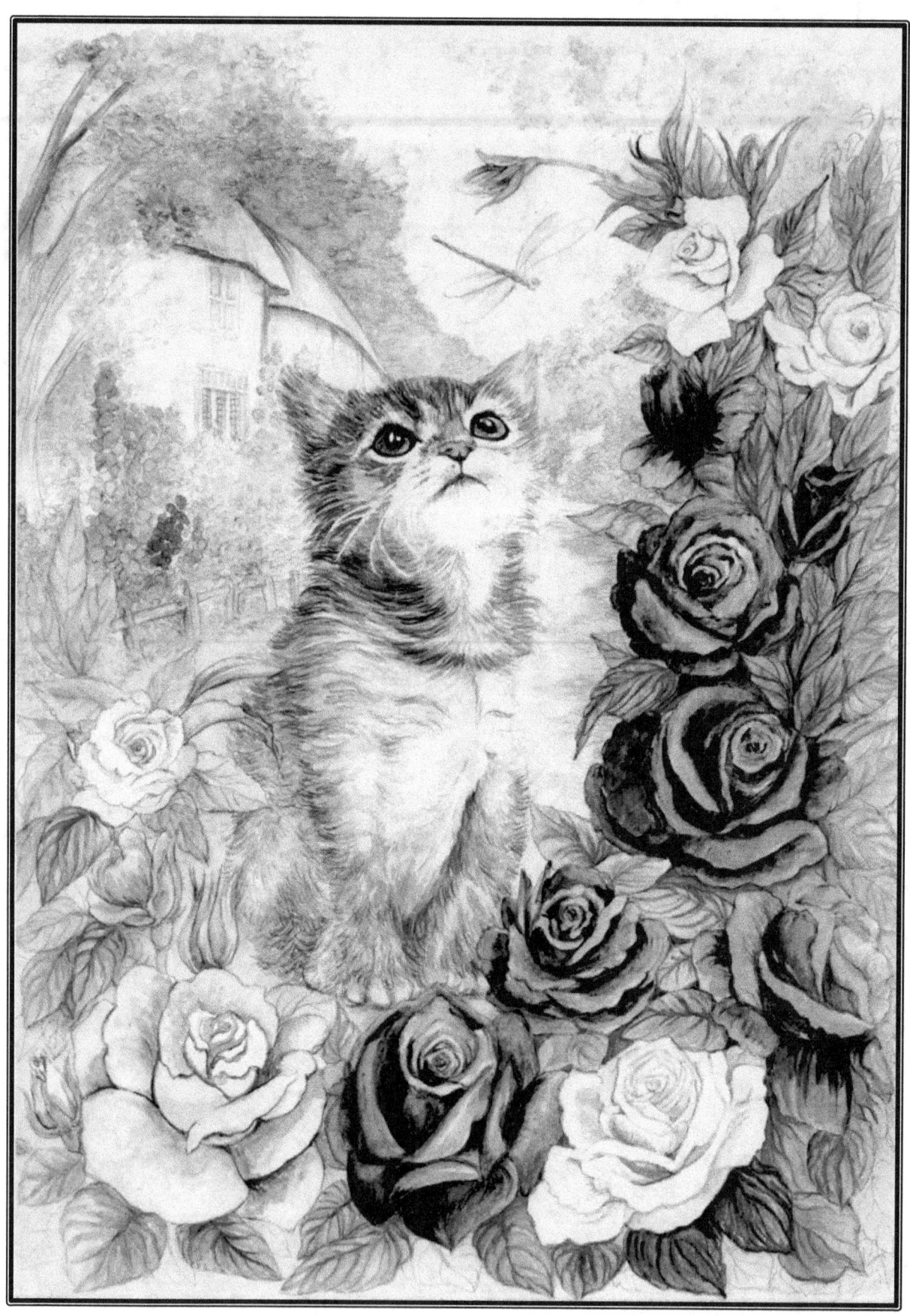

*Kitten Love Colouring Book*

*Artwork By*
*Morgan Fitzsimons Author-Artist*

*Graphics Layout By*
*Linda Larson*

*© 2017 Morgan Fitzsimons*
*All Rights Reserved*

*No part of this book may be reproduced, stored in a retrieval system, or transmitted by any means without written permission of the author.*

*Published by Fae Entertainment & Fae Workshop*

ISBN #978-1-7750241-4-9

*Published and Printed in All Countries Worldwide*

Printed in Paperback

info@Fae-Entertainment.ca

www.MorganFitzsimons.com

www.FaeEntertainment.com

www.Fae-Entertainment.ca

www.ArtStampsStore.com

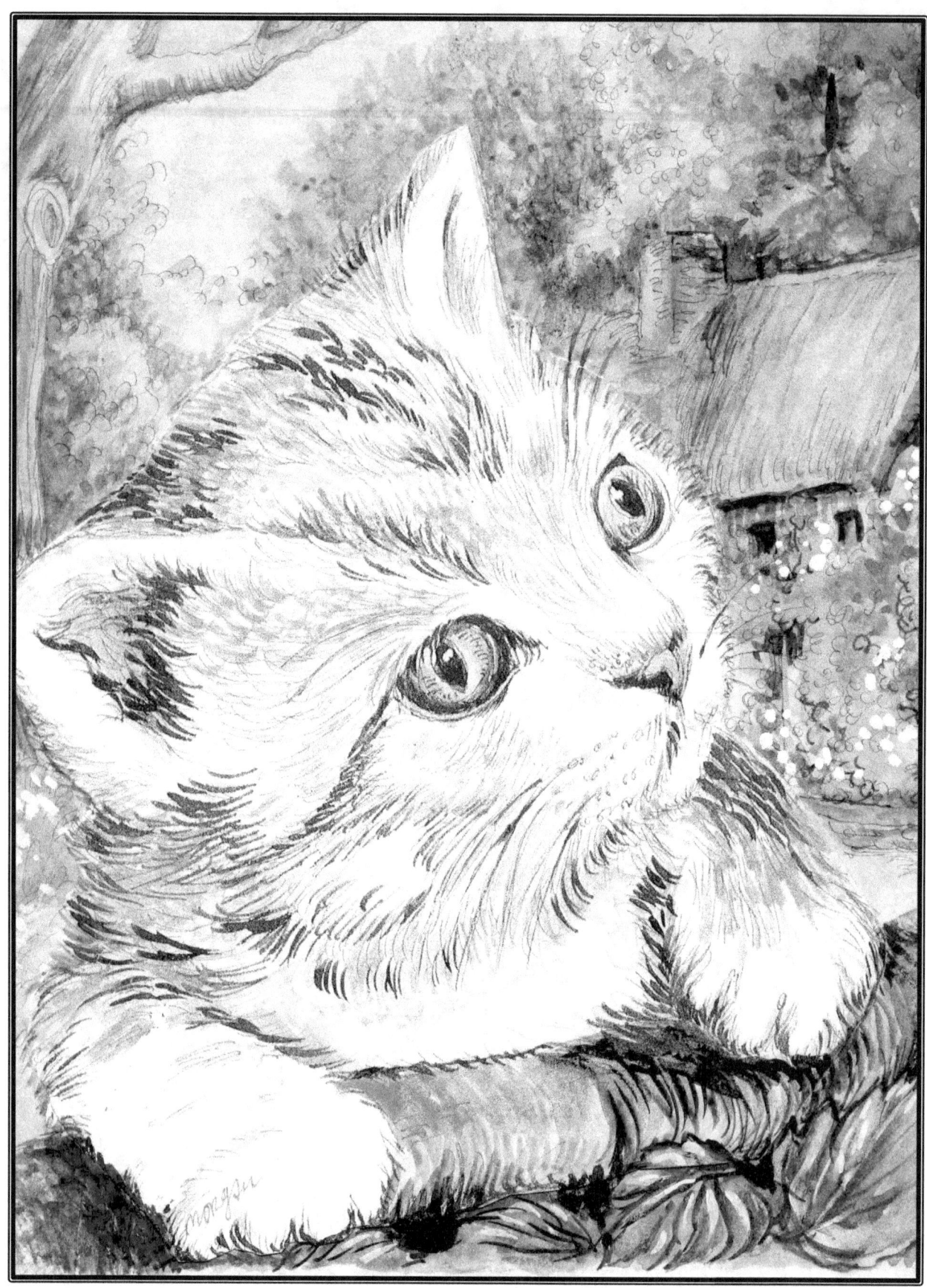

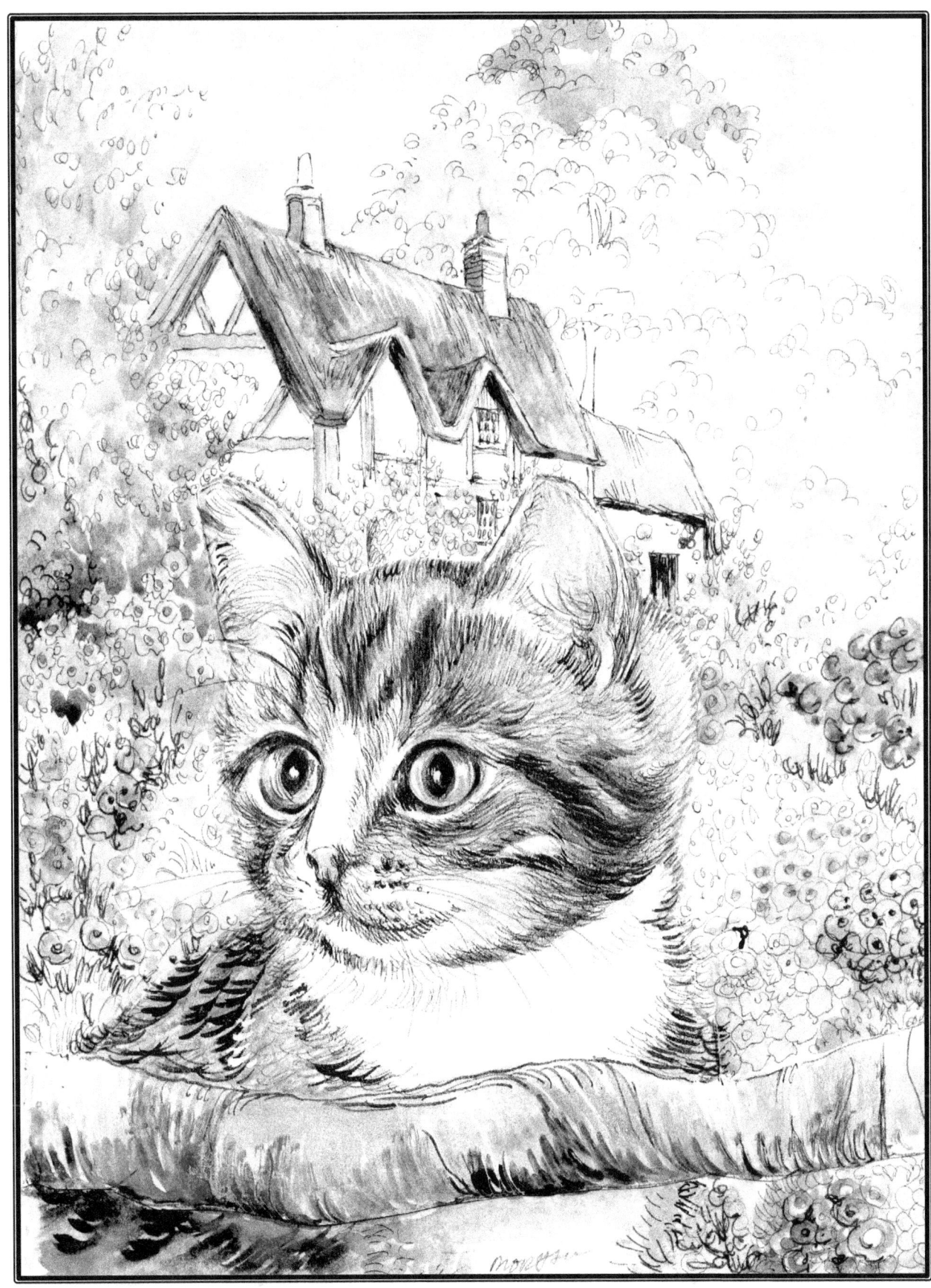

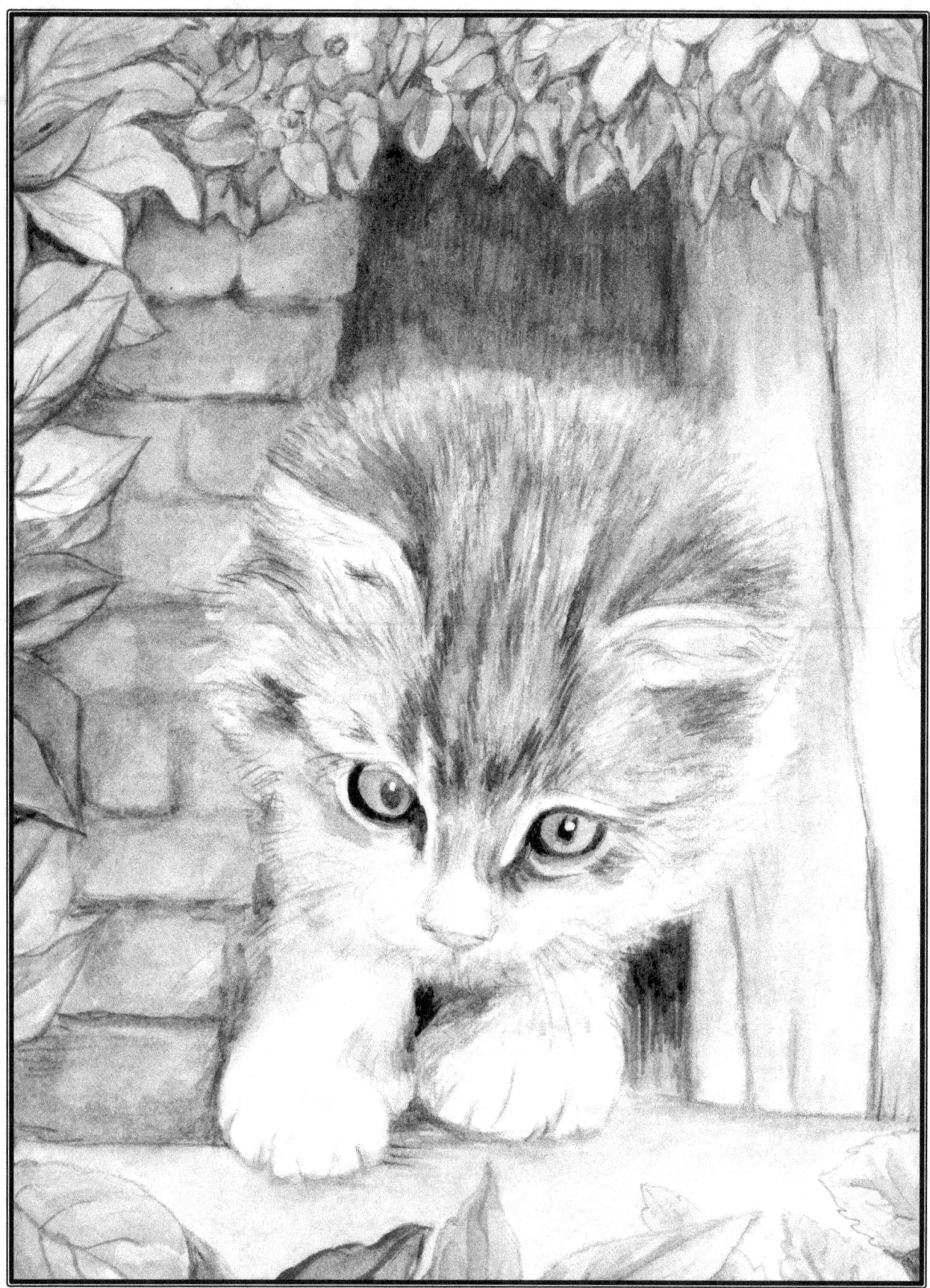

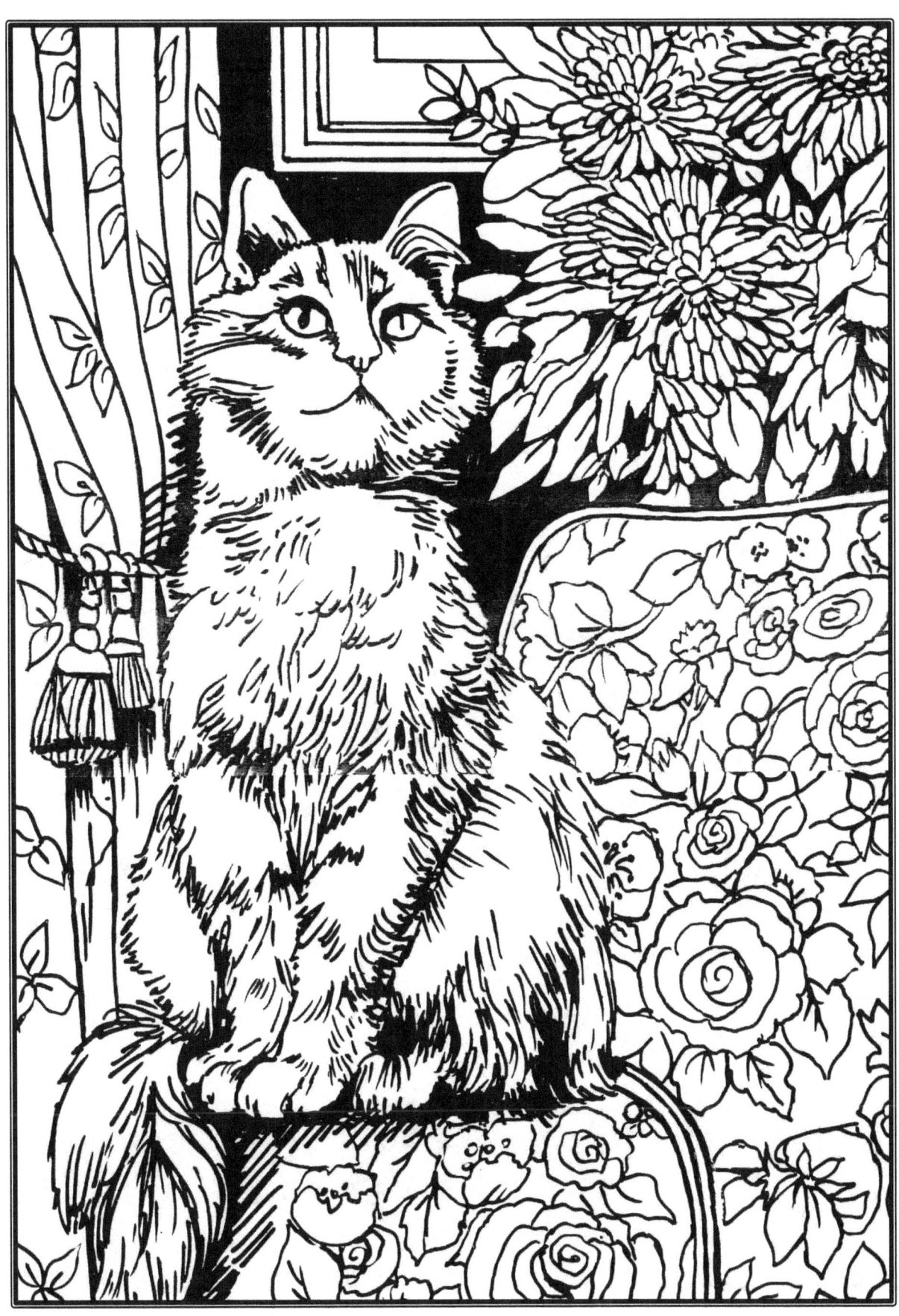

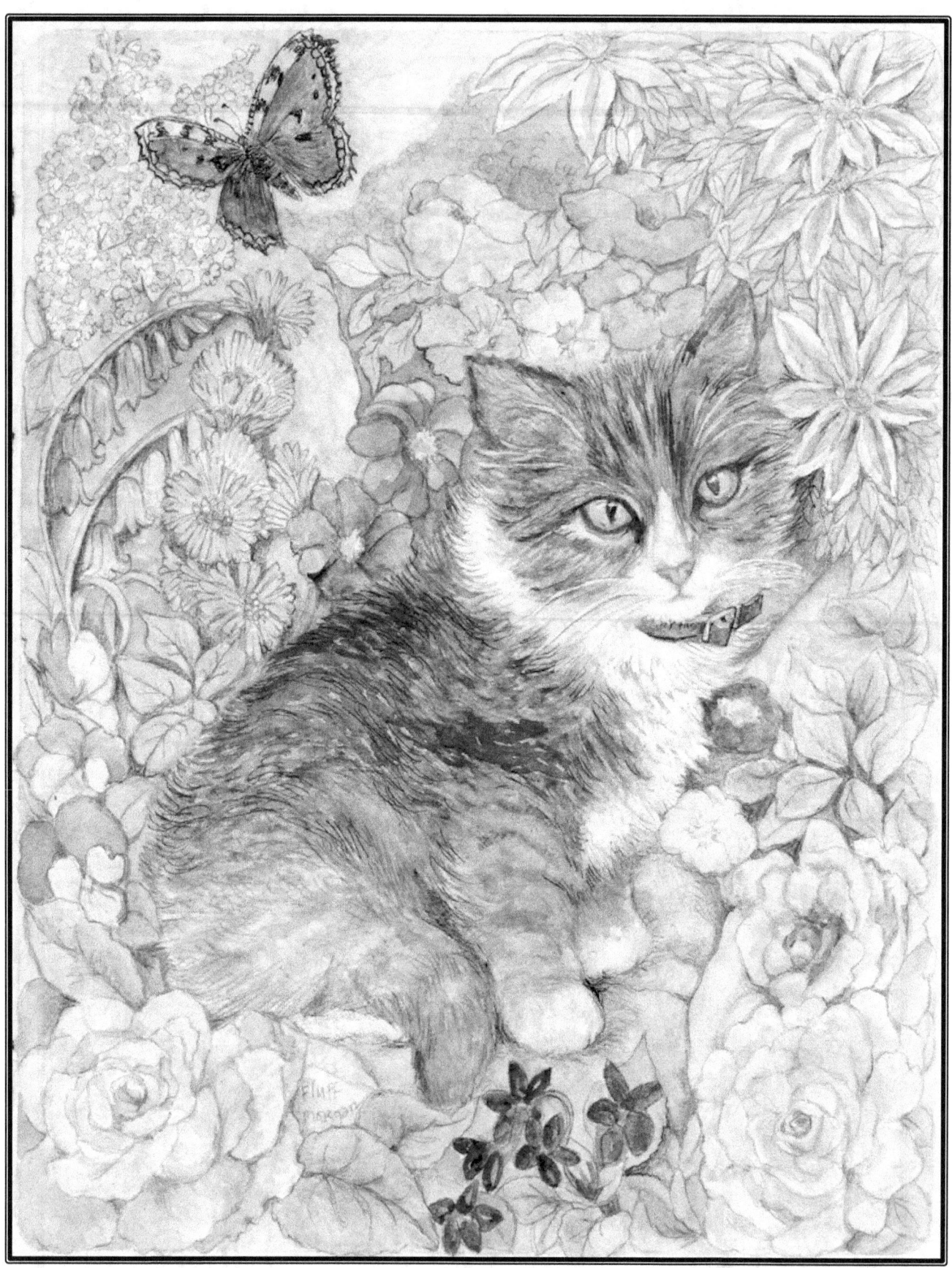

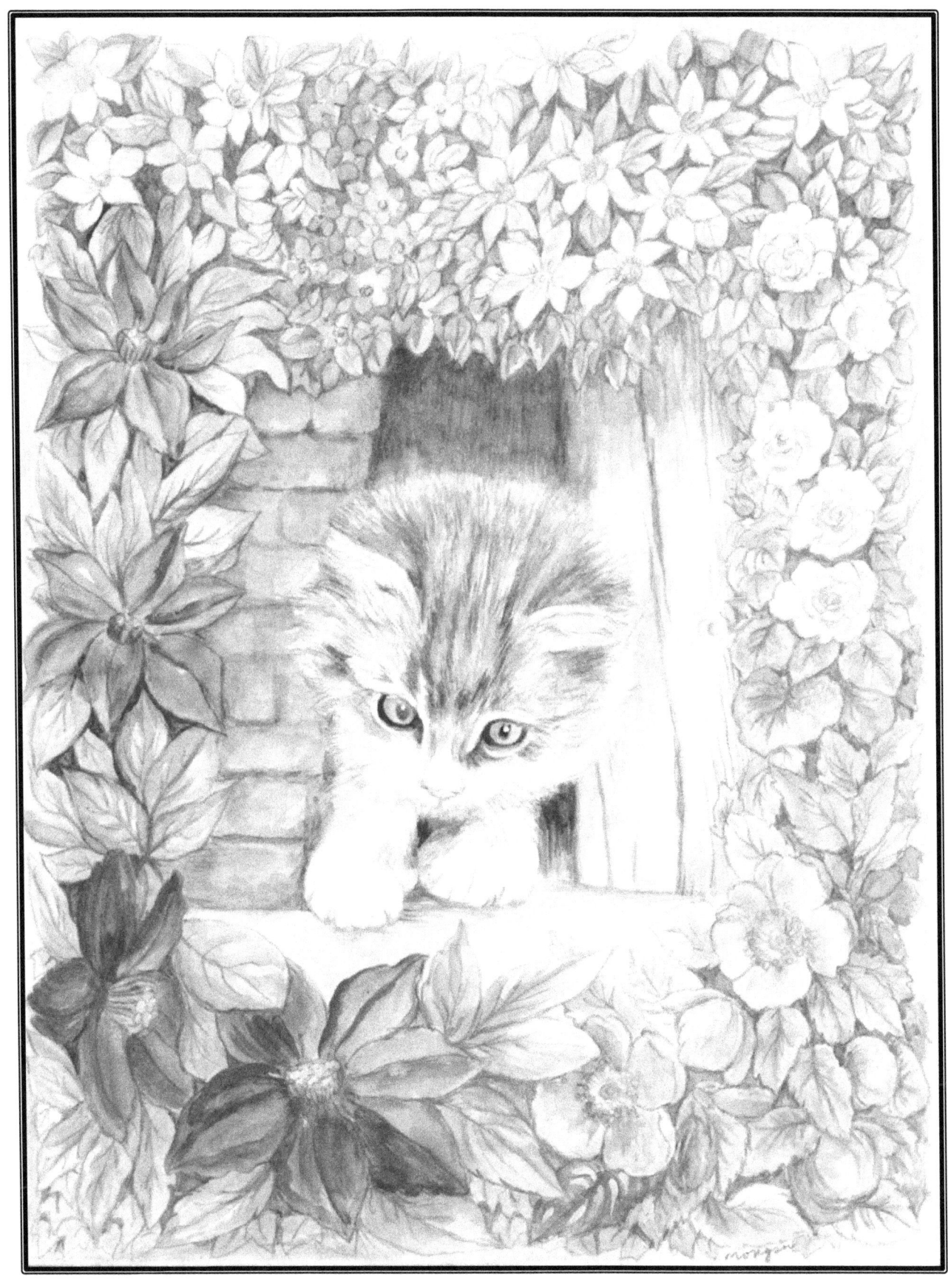

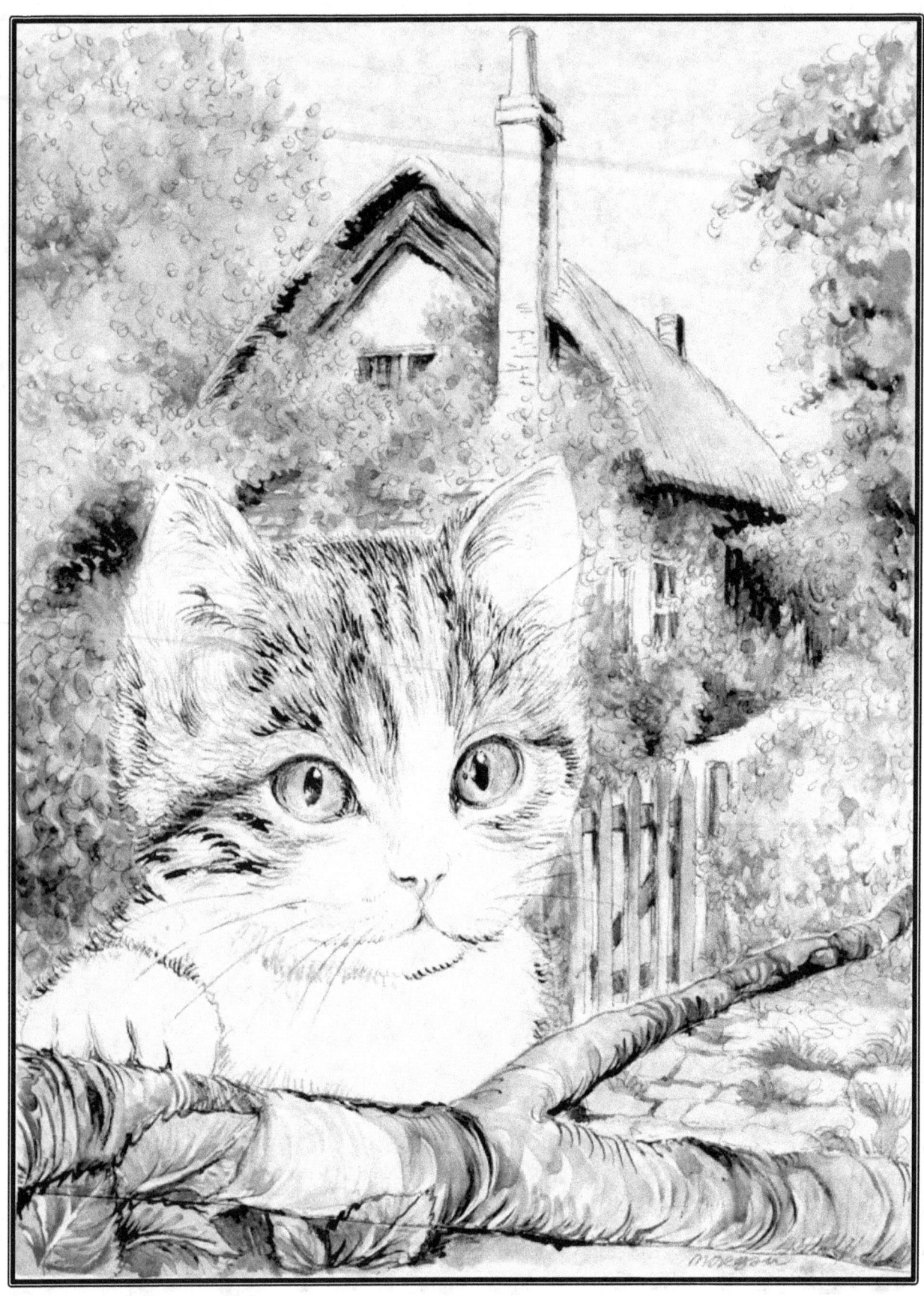

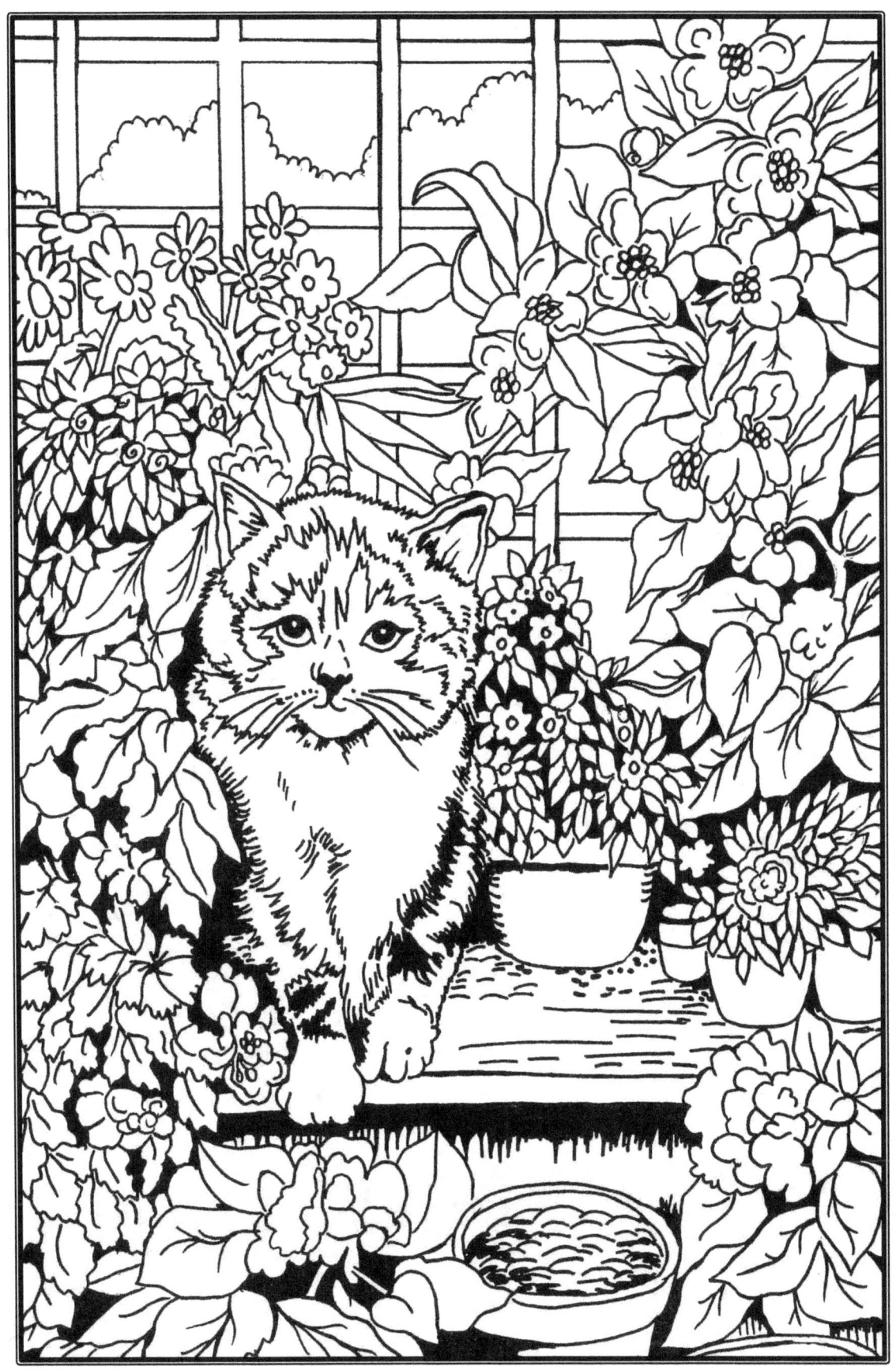

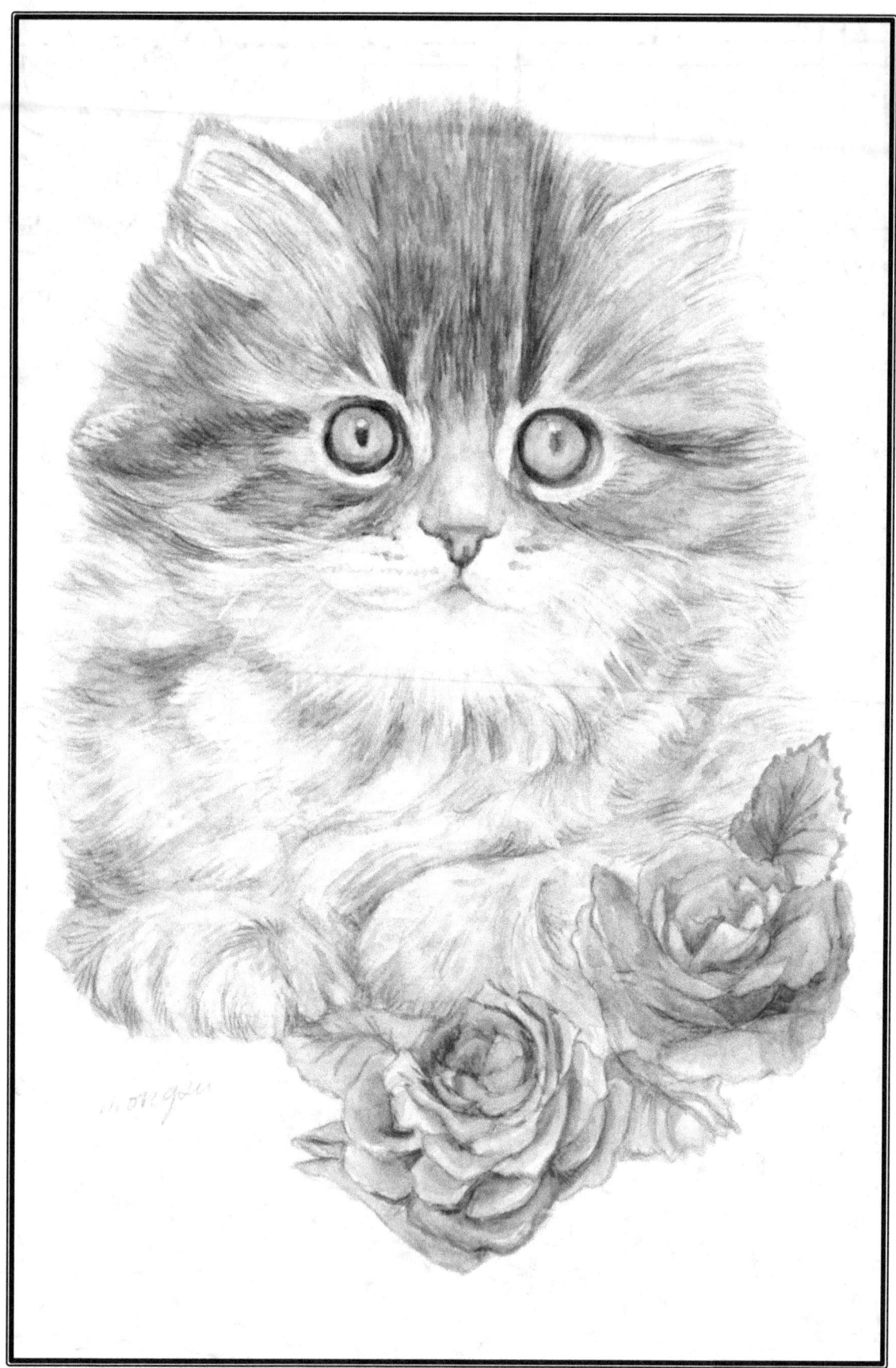

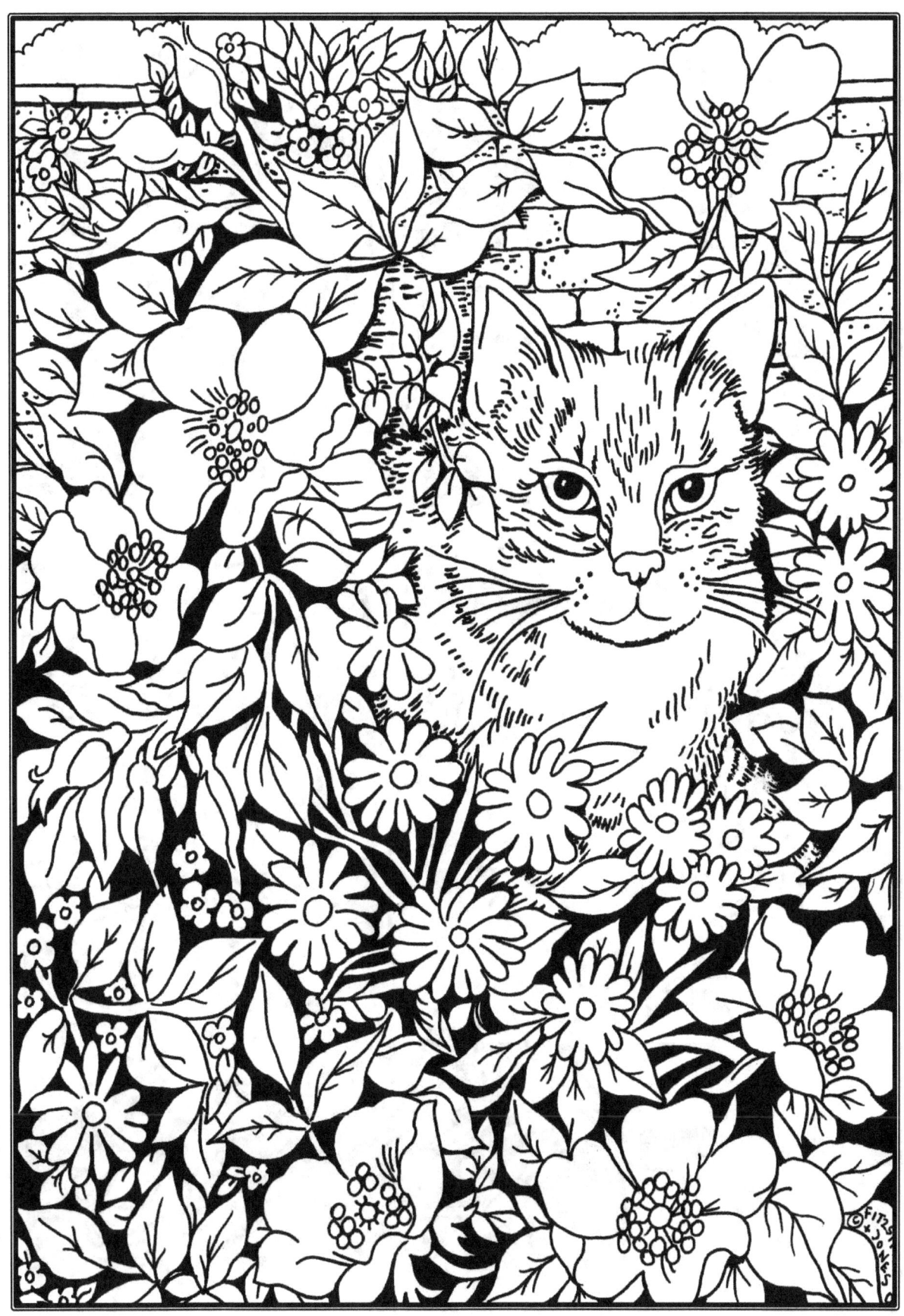

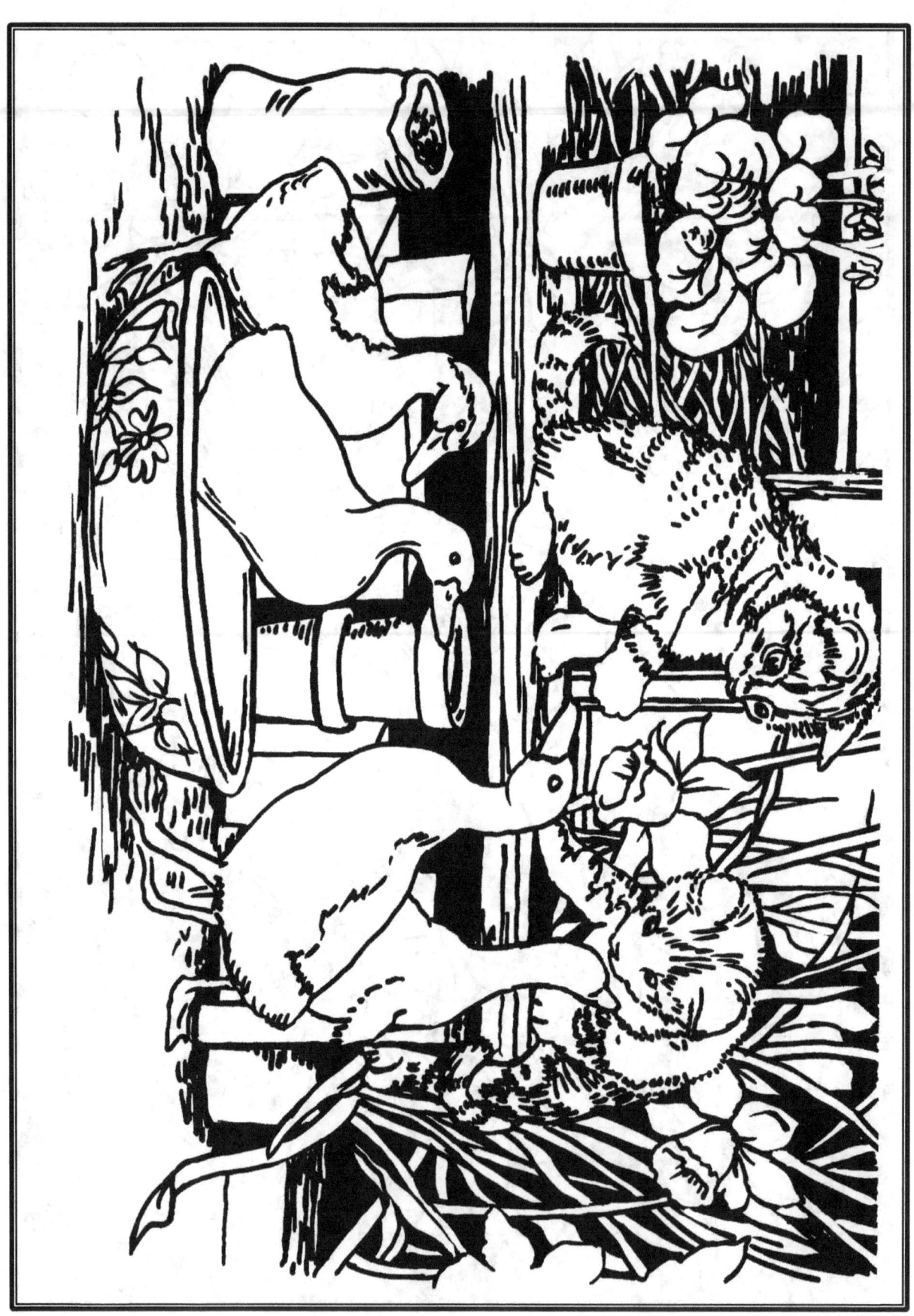

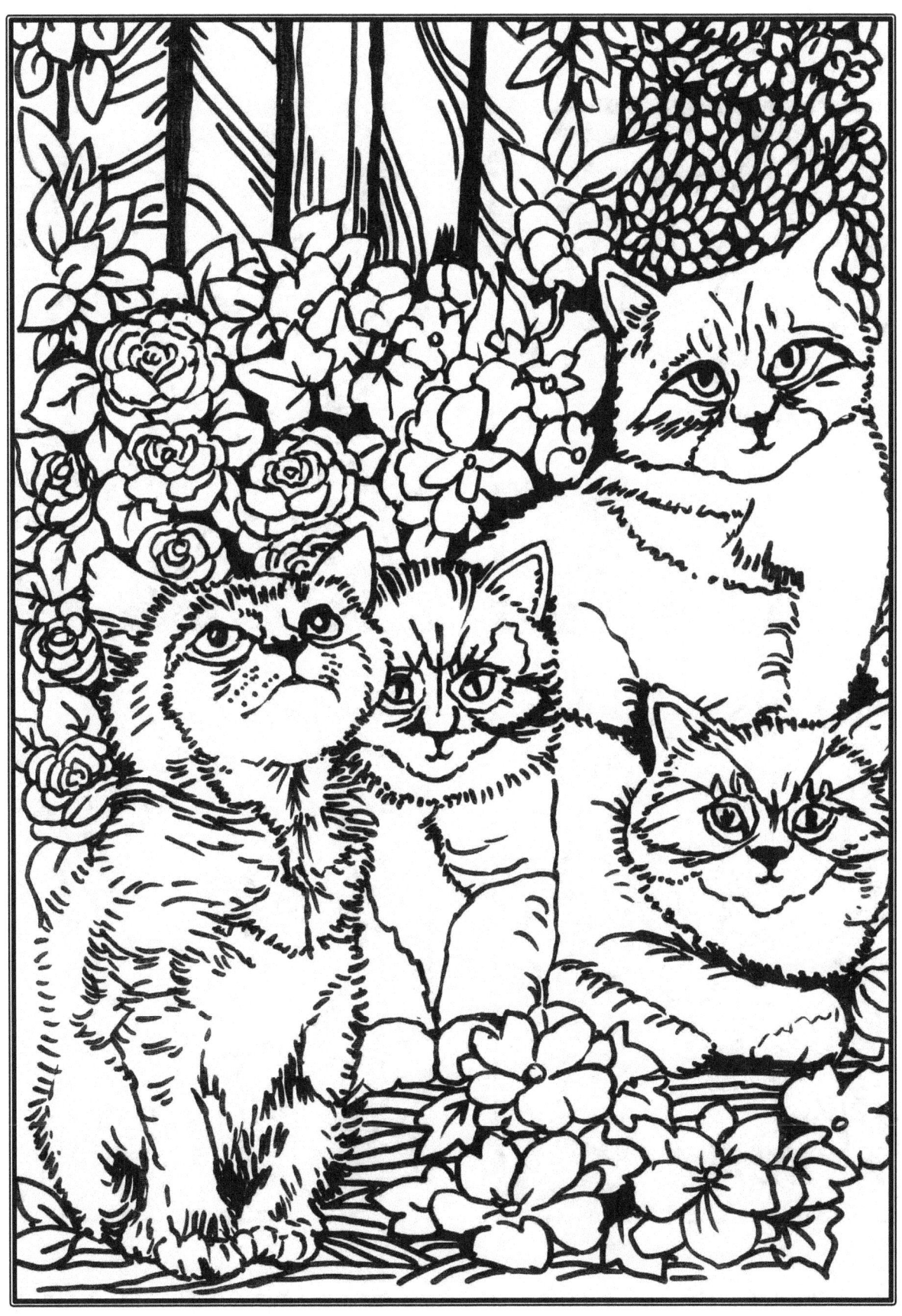

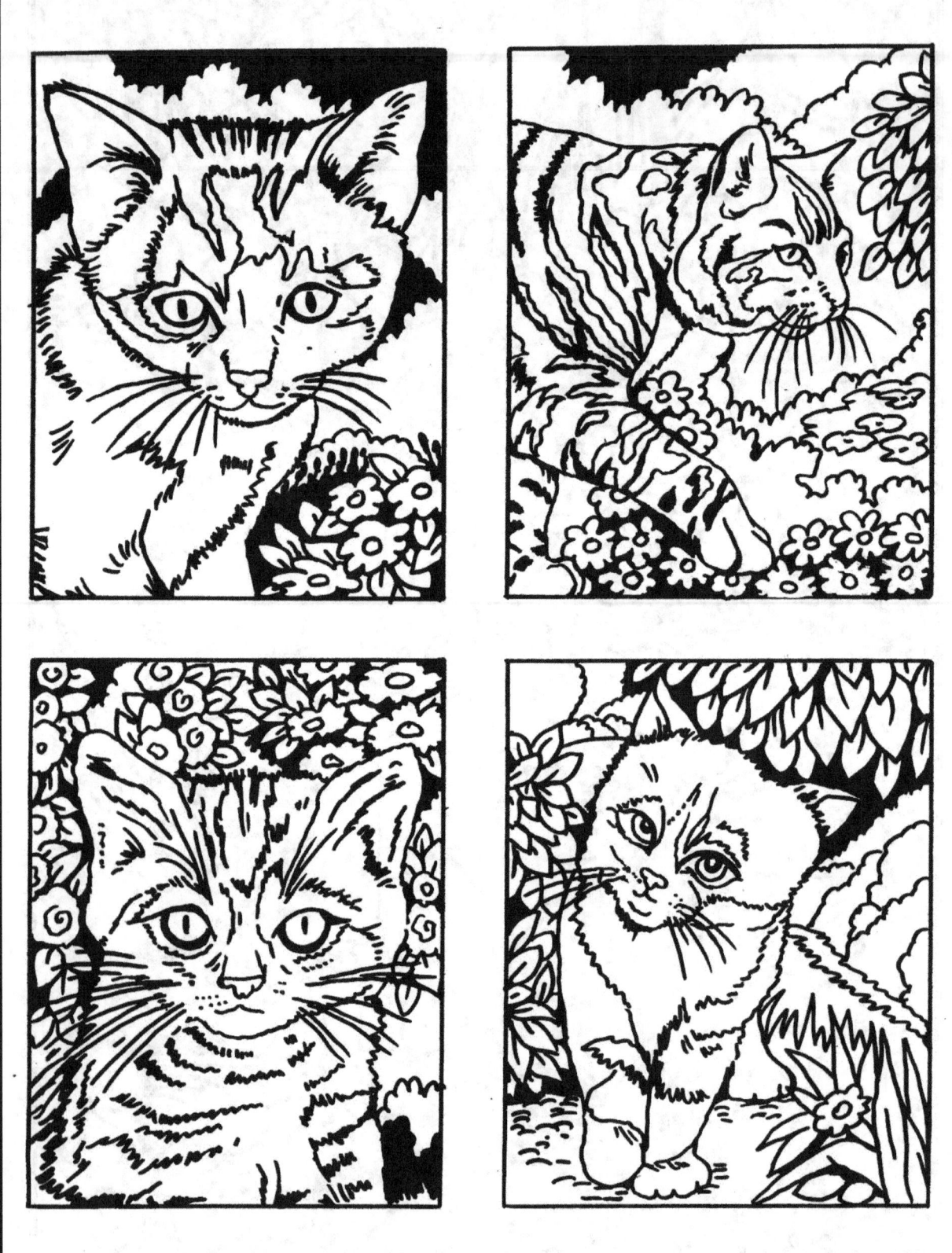

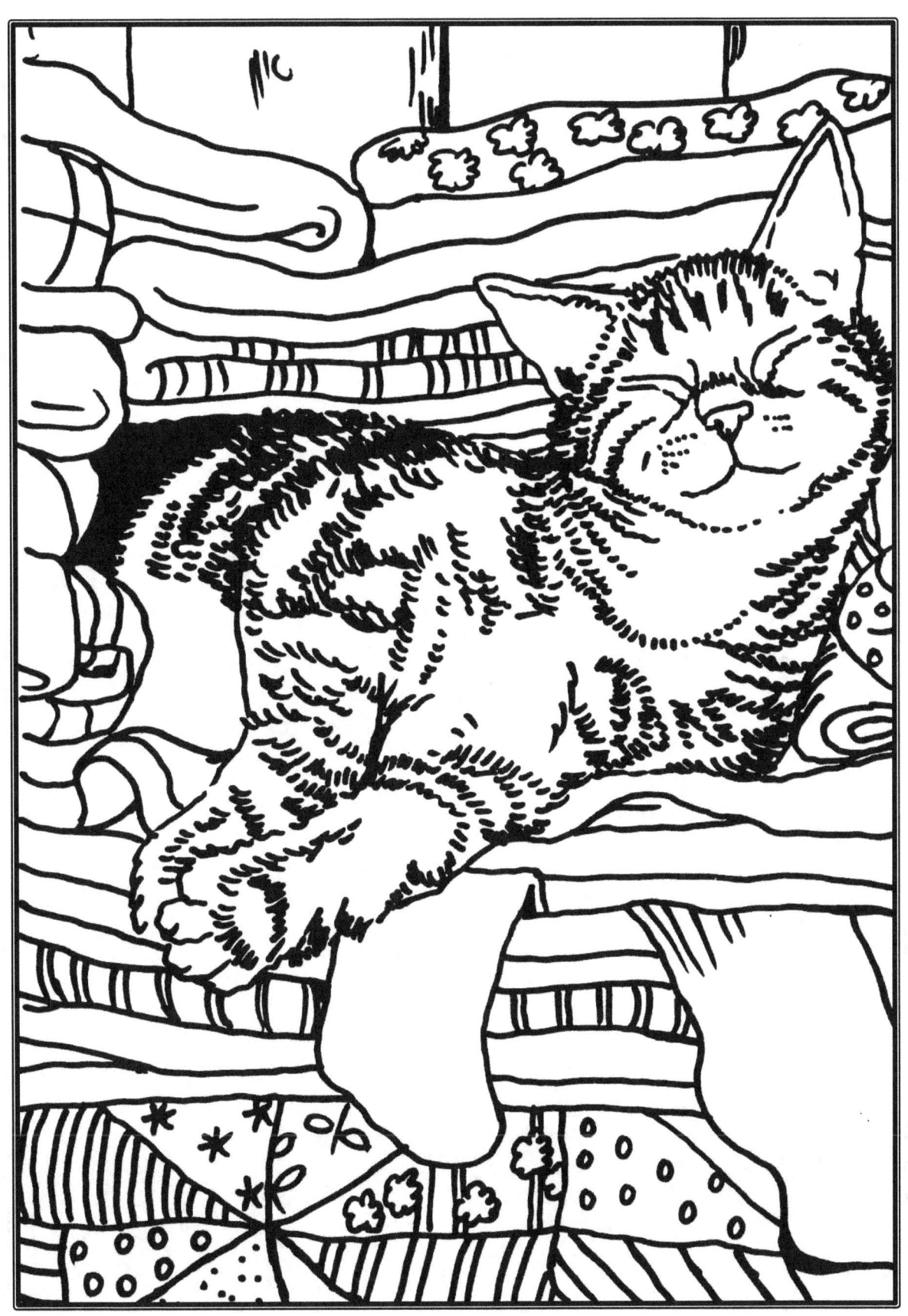

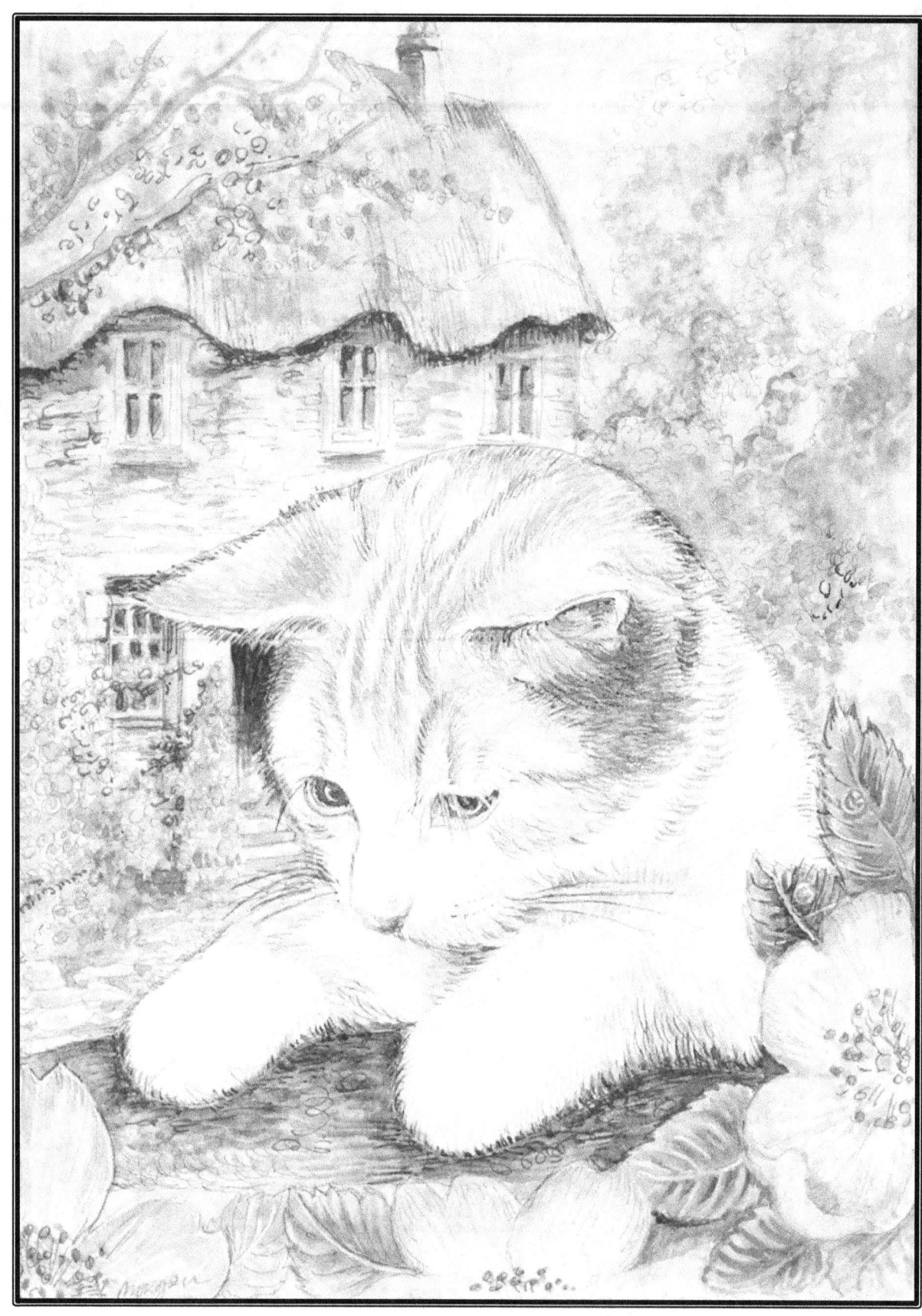

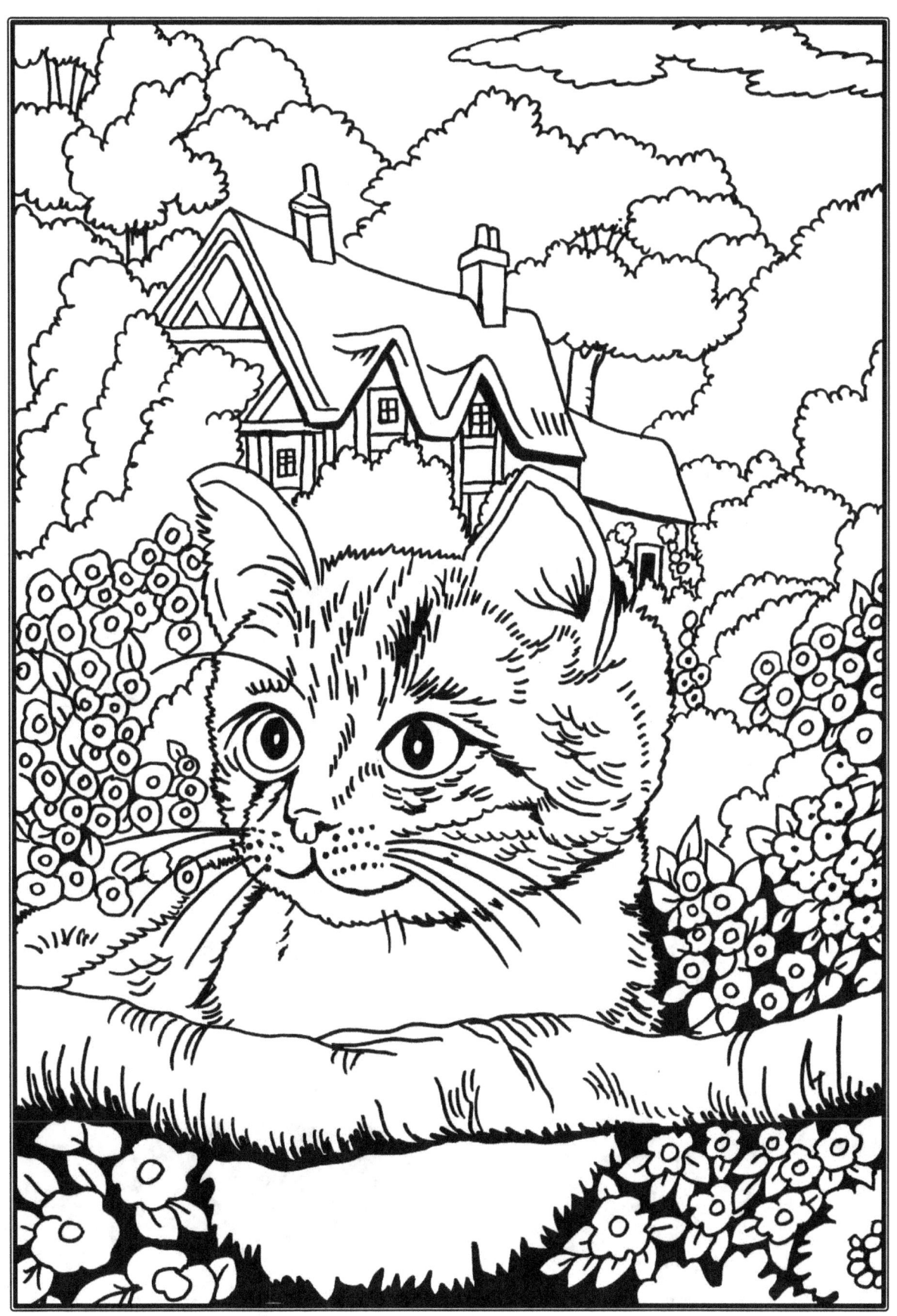

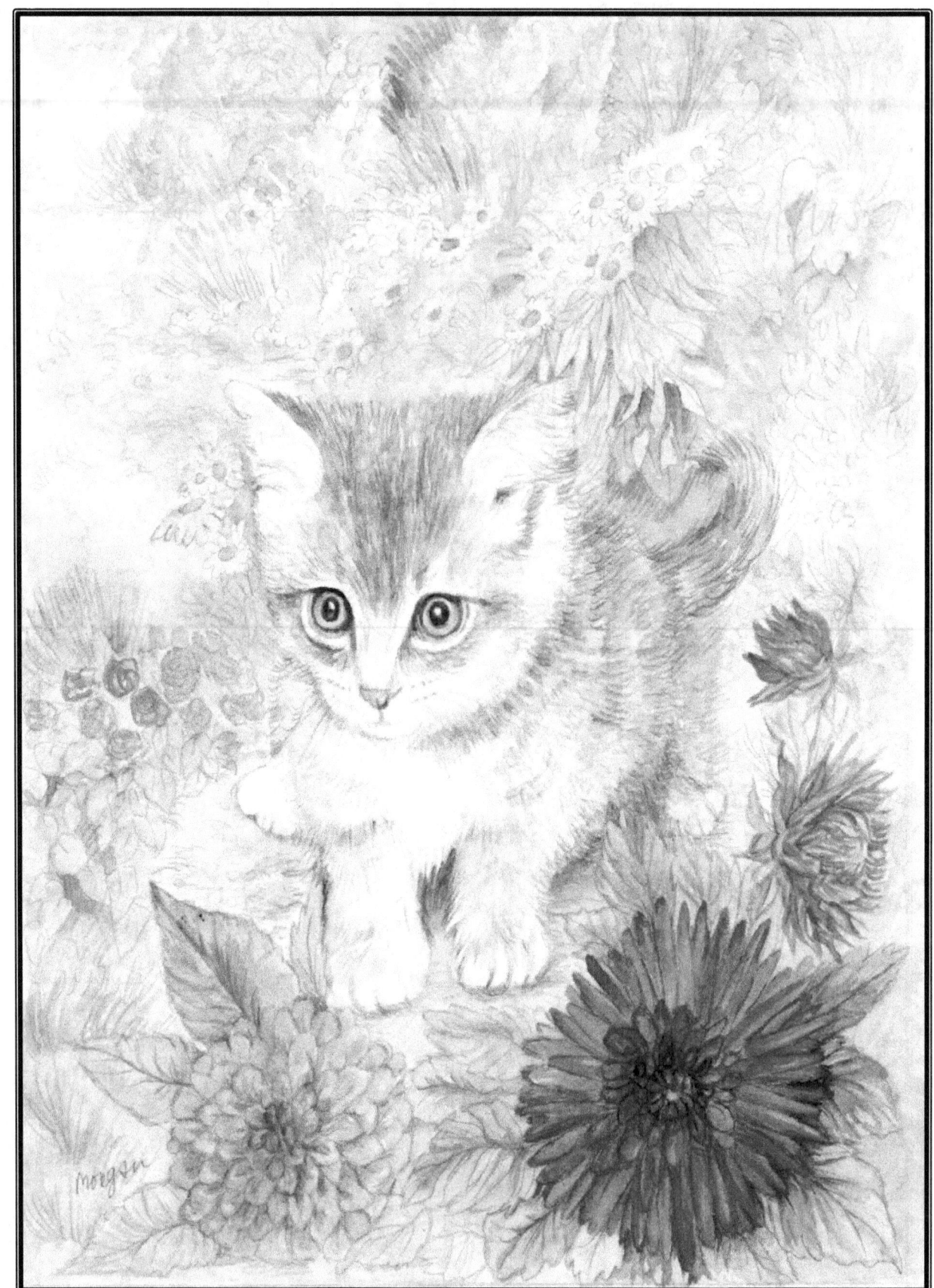

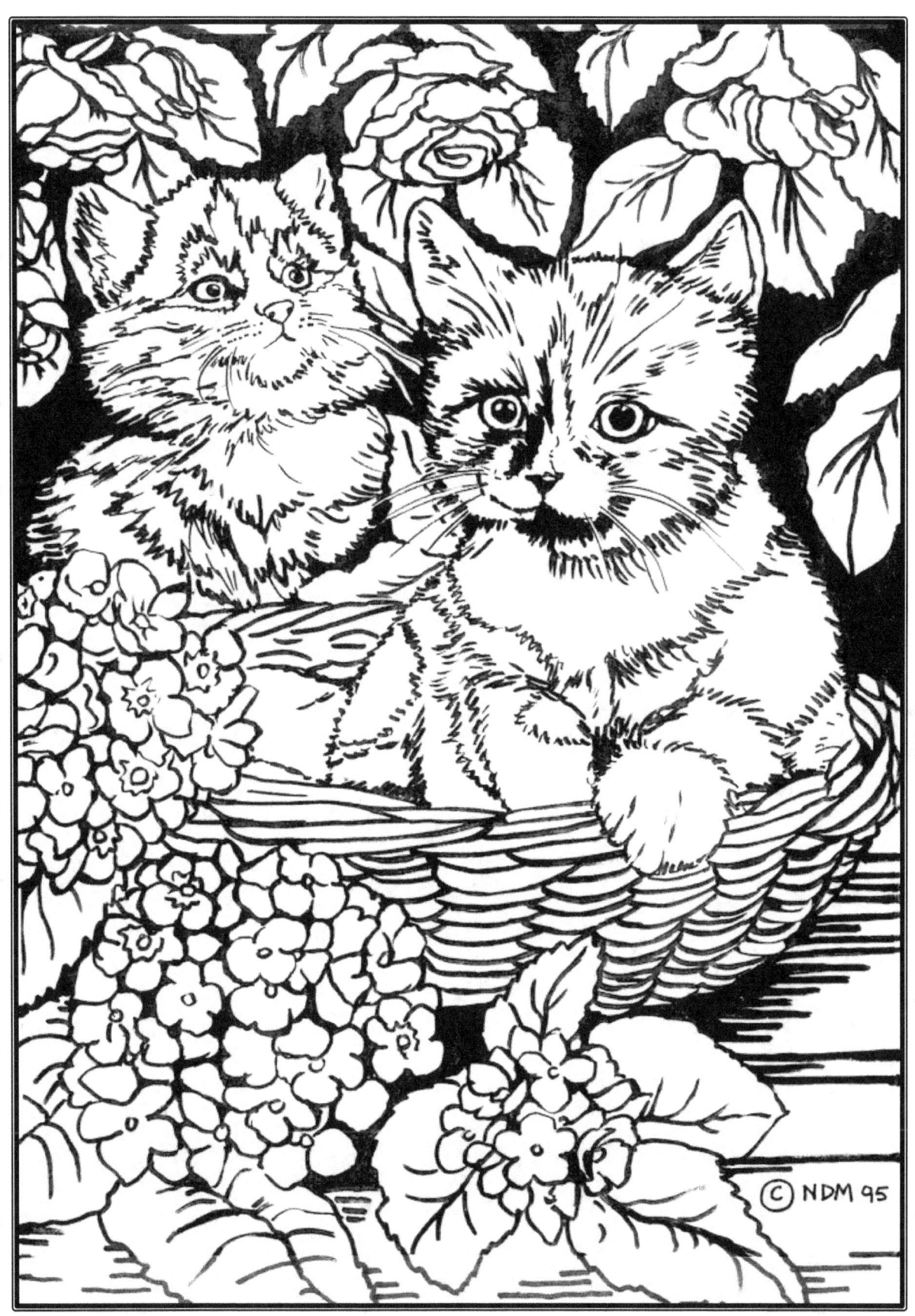

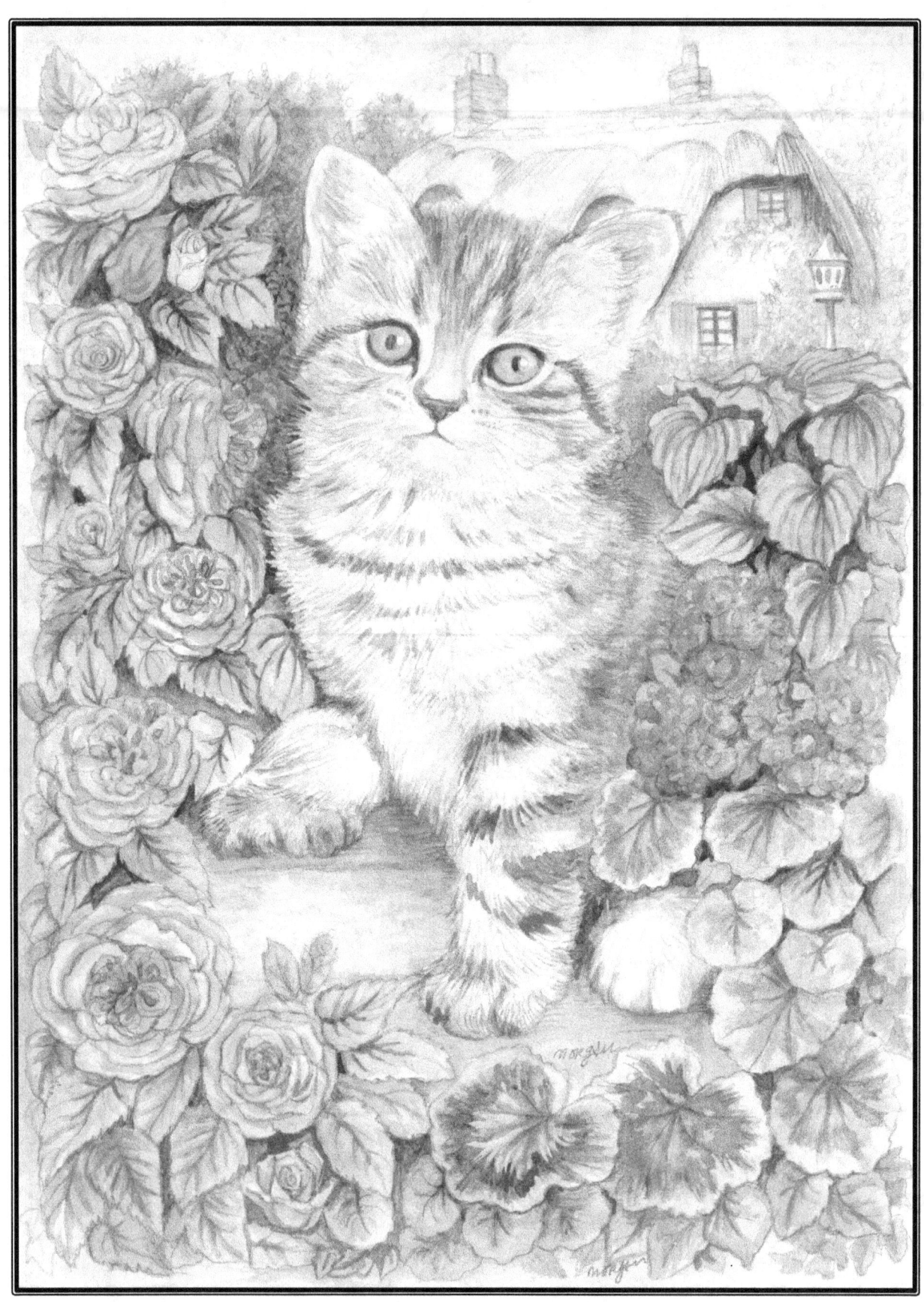

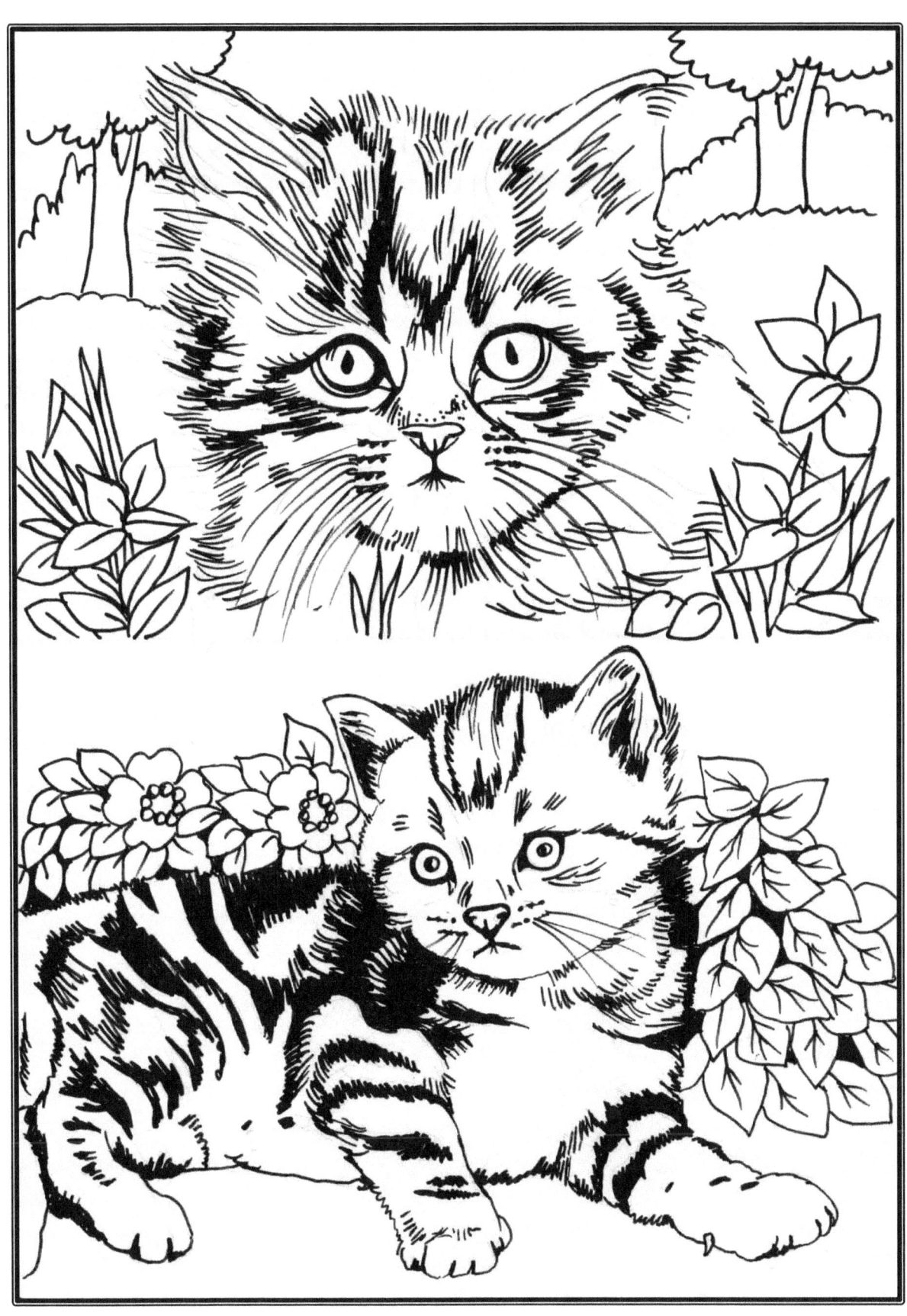

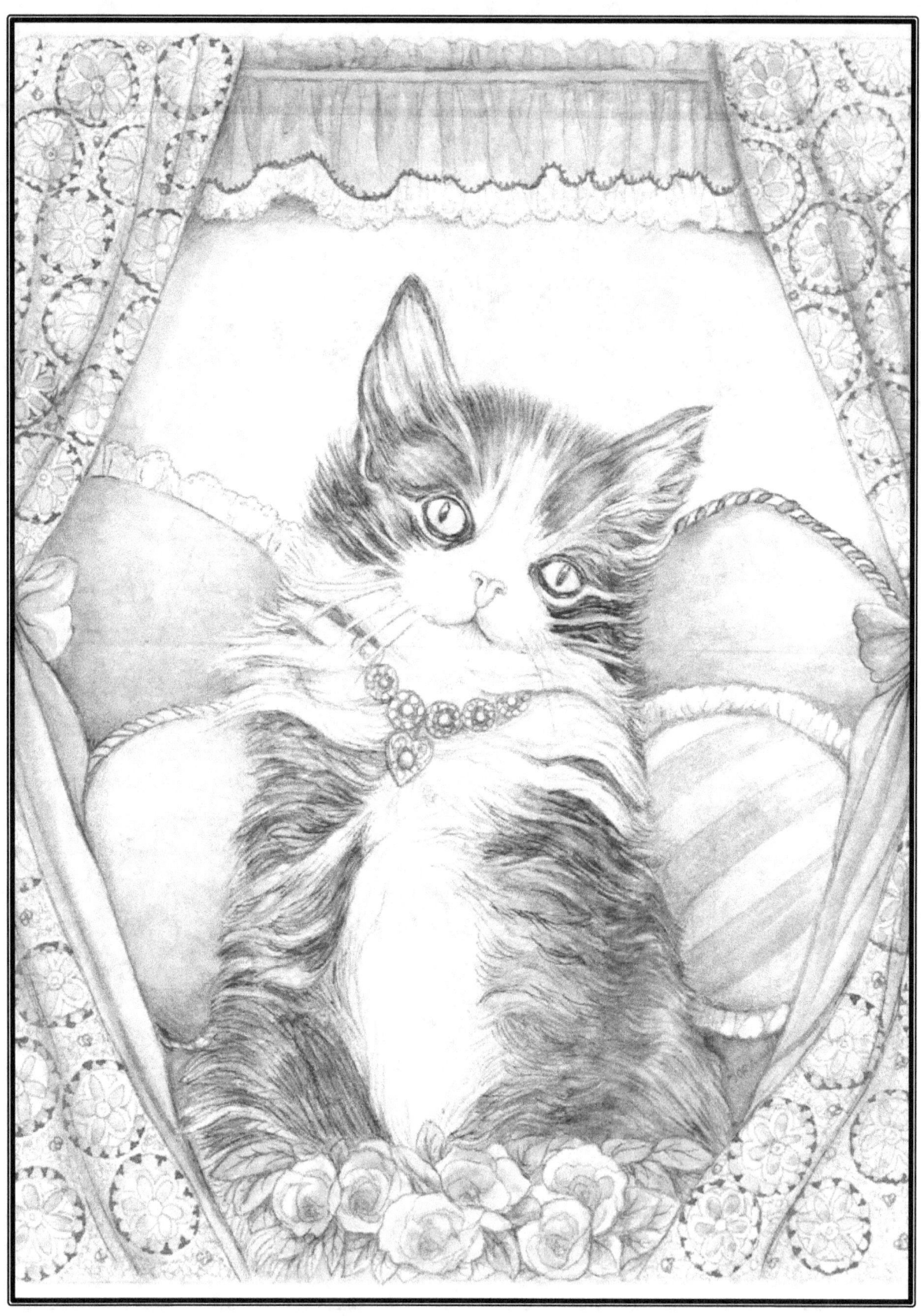

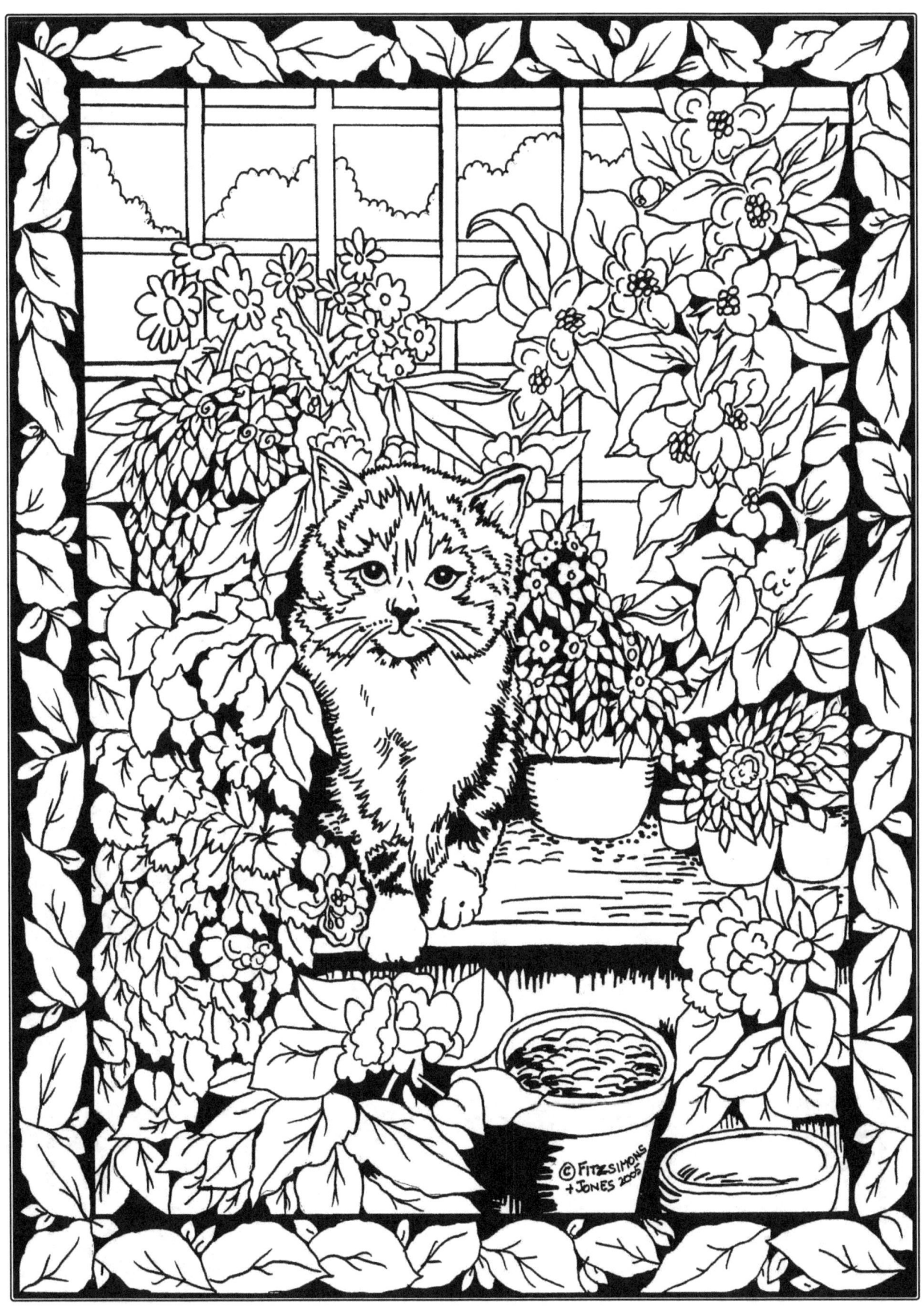

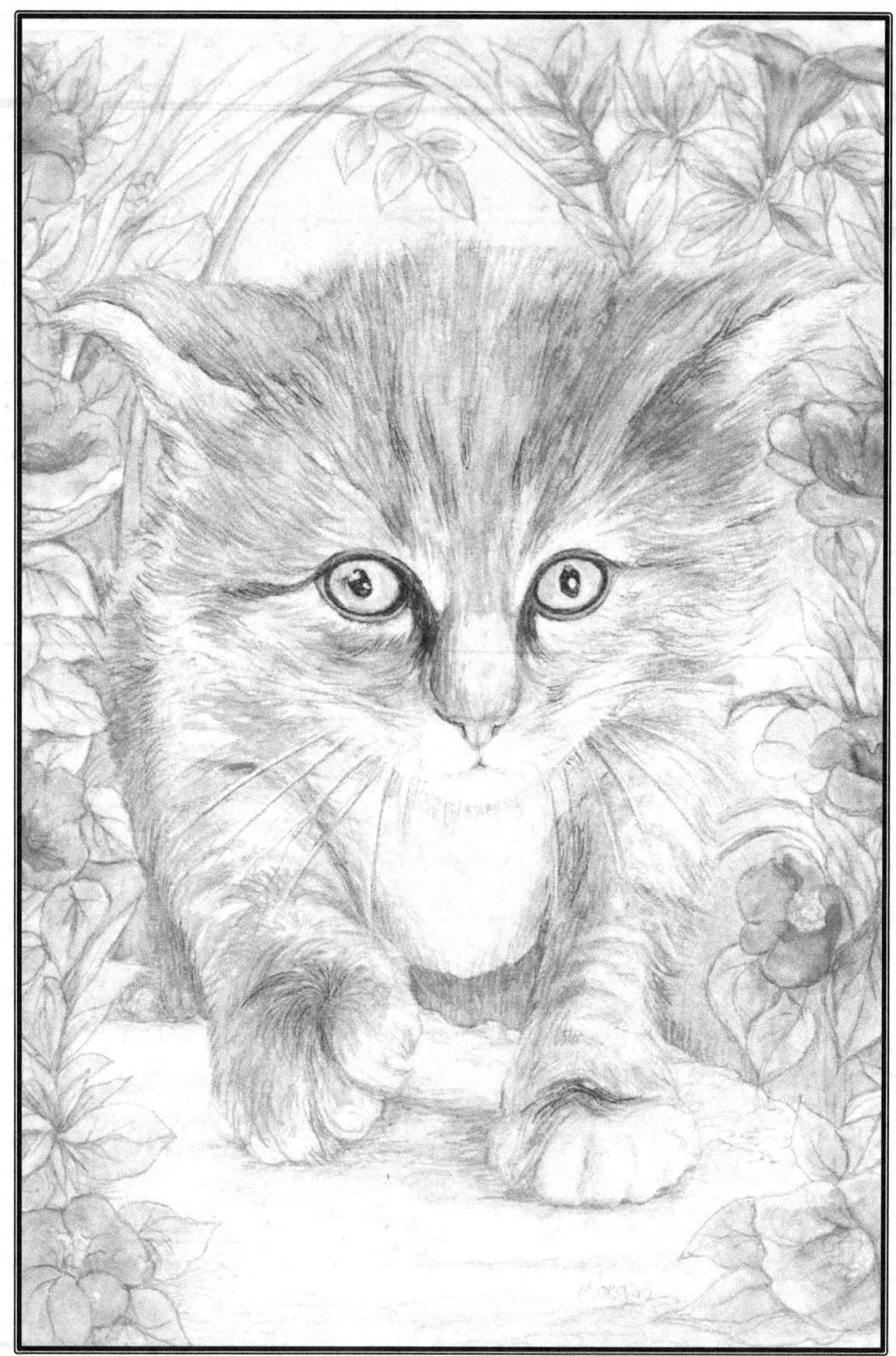

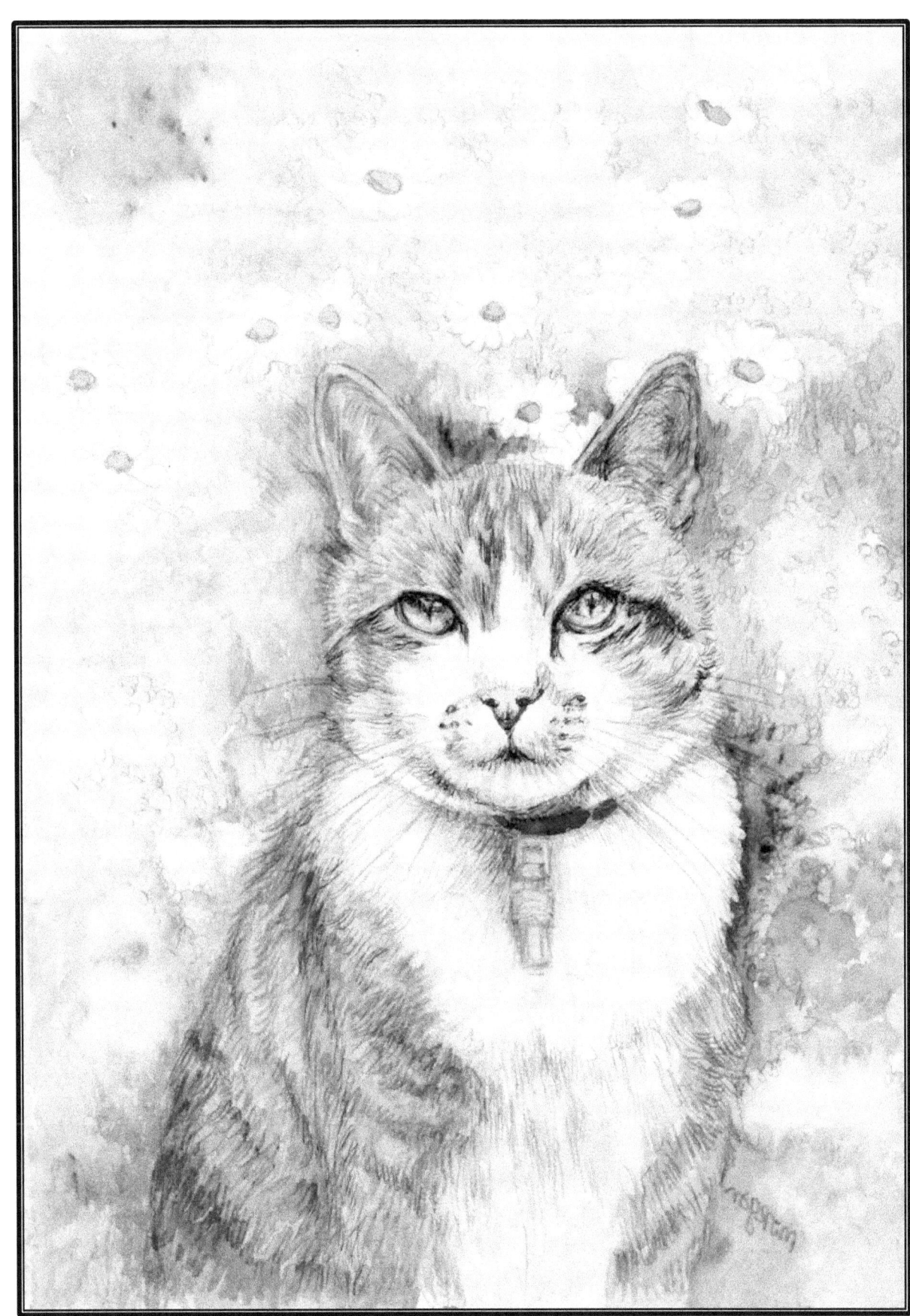

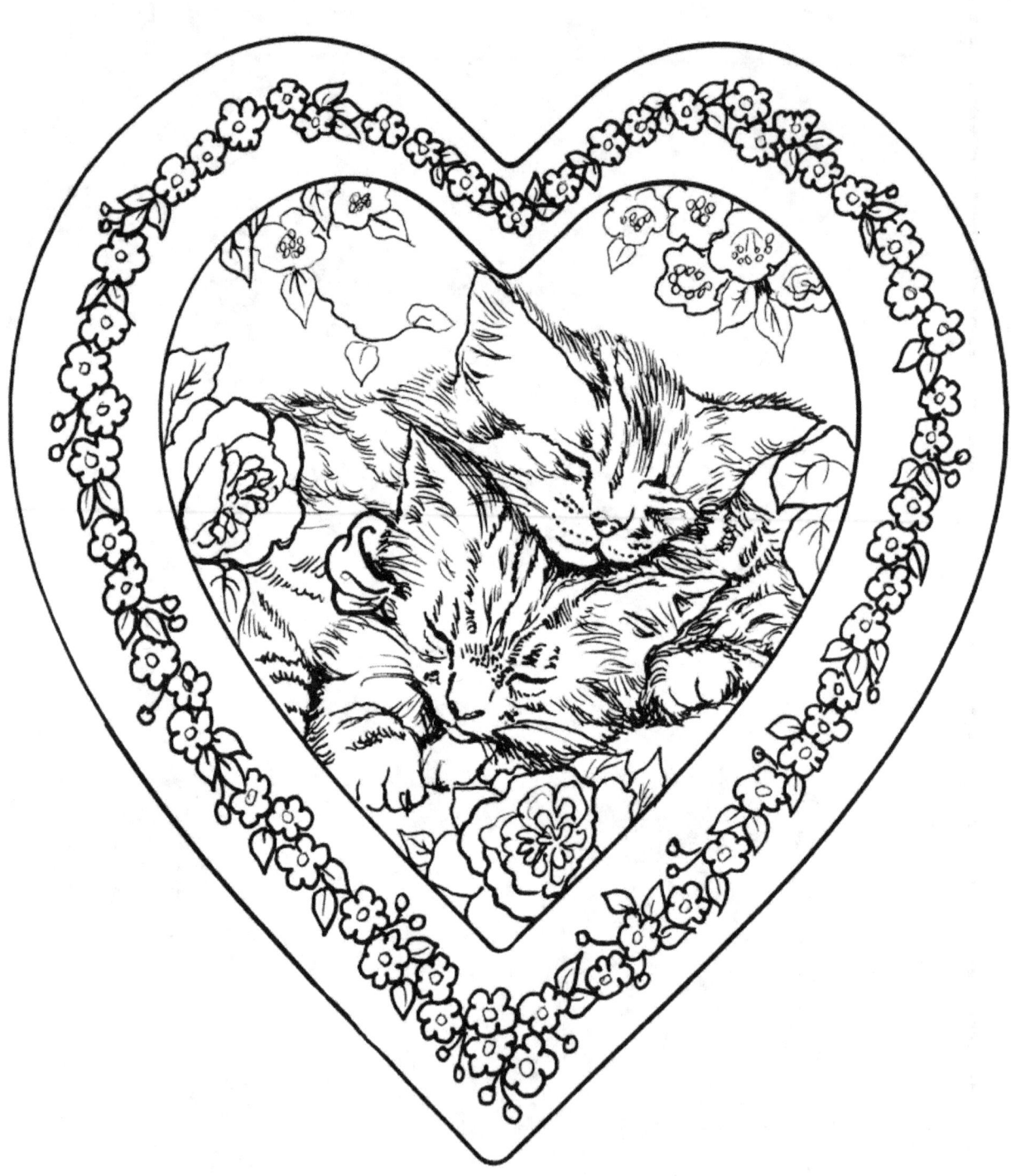